A Scroll Saw Christmas

Frank Pozsgai

Schiffer Publishing Ltd

77 Lower Valley Road, Atglen, PA 19310

D1717234

Contents

The Sleigh and Reindeer 4
   Wiring the Nose 15
   Painting the Sleigh 22
The Larger Deer 25
   Painting the Deer 27
The Gallery 30
Patterns for the Sleigh and Reindeer 33
The Storage Box 36
   Storage Box Plan 37
Ornament Patterns 38

Printed in China
ISBN: 0-88740-786-2

Library of Congress Cataloging-in-Publication Data

Pozsgai, Frank.
    A scroll saw Christmas: step-by-step to a 3-D sleigh & reindeer.
      p. cm.
    ISBN 0-88740-786-2 (paper)
    1. Jig saws. 2. Woodwork--Patterns. 3. Christmas decorations. I. Congdon-Martin, Douglas. II. Title.
TT186.P6913 1995
745.594'12--dc20
                    95-19424
                    CIP

Book Design by Audrey L. Whiteside.

Published by Schiffer Publishing, Ltd.
77 Lower Valley Road
Atglen, PA 19310
Please write for a free catalog.
This book may be purchased from the publisher.
Please include $2.95 postage.
Try your bookstore first.

We are interested in hearing from authors
with book ideas on related subjects.

Introduction

Nearly every body loves Christmas, and scroll sawyers are no exception! I know this is true because for a number of years I have had a hard time keeping up with the demand for the pattern of Santa and the Reindeer. Maybe it's the beloved Rudolph, who leads the sled, or maybe it's the music box that plays his song, but whatever, scroll sawyers and their families are drawn to this project.

This book is designed to introduce the scroll sawyer to the joys of 3-dimensional work. Too many of us seem locked into working "flat," cutting pictures and other 2-dimensional projects, which, while beautiful, do not use the full capabilities of the saw.

Three-dimensional work is more demanding, but only a little bit. With a few special techniques, the world of the scroll expands exponentially. Suddenly you are able to do things that once seemed impossible. It will make a beautiful Christmas fixture on your fireplace mantle, coffee table, or credenza.

I hope that the 3-dimensional "miracle" will be part of your Christmas work, and that you enjoy this book as much as I have enjoyed preparing it.

The Sleigh and Reindeer

Items Needed

1 Santa Claus Figure
1 Red Blinking LED
1 Roll of Wrapping Wire
1 Electronic Music Box that plays "Rudolph"

The reindeer and sleigh require three "non-wood" items, a flashing LED for Rudolph's nose, an electronic music box that plays "Rudolph the Red Nose Reindeer," and a Santa Claus. The first two items can be found at many craft stores or by contacting me at 19390 S.W. Murphy, Aloha, OR 97007-4428 (Telephone: 503-642-3850; fax 503-649-7791). The Santa Claus is harder to find, but I have had some luck at stores that specialize in Christmas items. The one illustrated here was a Christmas tree ornament.

Added decorative concepts can include cotton or angel hair on the base to simulate snow, and a harness to fit on the deer and reins that go into Santa's hands.

Wood

Choose whatever wood you like. The softer woods cut easier, but if you are going to paint the figure use pine. Walnut, oak or koa look beautiful for the deer with a clear acrylic spray.

The sleigh needs to be painted for a more aesthetic look. The base should be a nice piece of hardwood, although if you plan to cover it with cotton "snow" almost any wood will work.

Equipment

Scroll Saw
Hand drill and assorted bits
Solder and soldering gun
Rounter and router bits
Belt sander
Sand paper (220 grit)
Carpenter's glue
Krylon Acrylic Spray (clear)

Your Scroll Saw

Although we own a variety of saws, one common thing is that 98% of scroll saws have a 2" maximum cutting capacity. The others have a capacity of 1 3/4". If the patterns do not fit your saw, you will need to enlarge or reduce them on a copier.

For soft woods use a #5 blade (15 teeth to the inch) for this project. With hard woods use a FR420R in combination with a #9PGT. Make sure you have proper blade tension (rule of thumb: 1/8" deflection, front to rear, when pushing the blade with your thumb). Periodic blade tension adjustment is a must.

Cutting a 3-D pattern will certainly challenge even the best scroll saw operator. It truly requires concentration and strength. Remember to hold together all you pieces. Since there will be a lot of blade deflection, your best strokes/minute will be 1600 to 1800. DO NOT OVERFEED YOUR BLADE! Allow your cut to be straight. Your result will be greater per pattern. Another tip: make several photocopies of your pattern, then use a glue stick on the back of the paper and stick it directly onto the wood you'll be cutting.

Good luck and have fun with this project!

For the base of the sleigh and reindeer I have chosen a red oak, primarily for its color. It is 3/4" thick stock.

Cut the board to a length of 28".

It will be 3 1/2" wide, so I set the fence on the table saw to that width.

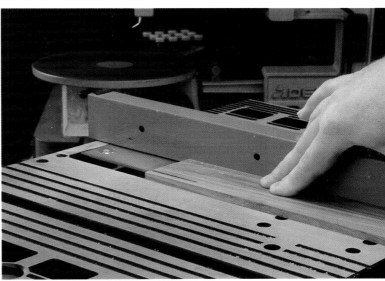

The sub-base which goes beneath the reindeer, is 2 1/2" x 14" x 1/4" and is of black walnut to contrast with the lighter oak. Cut to dimension.

Rip the length.

The underside of the sub-base has a channel cut down the center to hide the wires. It is about 1/16" deep. Set the saw blade for that depth and the fence at 1 1/4", and run the sub-base over the saw.

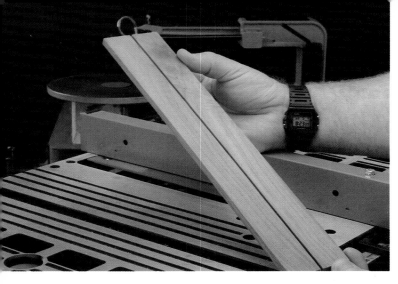

The result.

The same bit is used on the base to make a hole for the music box. The hole is centered 17 1/4" from the front edge of the board. It is 1/2" deep.

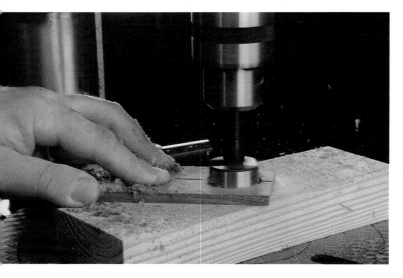

At one end of the sub-base use a 1 1/2" Forstner bit to make a shallow hole to hold excess wire. Again, it will be about 1/16" deep. Set a stop in the drill press so you don't go too deep.

The result.

The result.

Use a 7/64" bit to drill a hole in the sub-base where the wire will enter Rudolph's leg. From the front edge of the sub-base measure 2 1/2"...

6

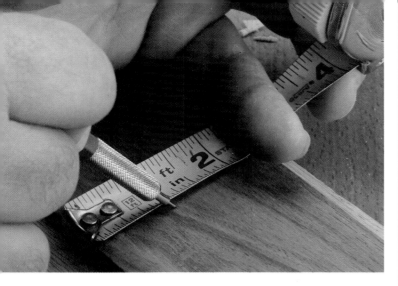

and from the left side measure 1 1/8".

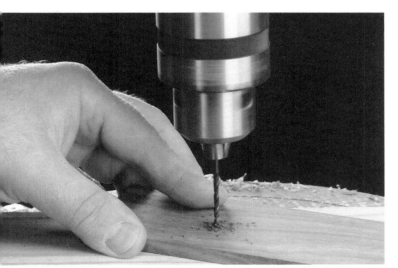

Drill the hole.

Use a round-over router bit to round the edges of the sub-base.

Continue on all sides.

On the base I am using an ogee bit, but you can use any decorative shape you like. Take the router all around the base.

Photocopy the pattern from the book. I cut the blocks for the deer to measure 5 1/4" long x 2" wide x 3/4"+ thick. I usually run one edge on a joiner before cutting to length to insure that the cross cuts are nice and square. This will help the deer stand steady. I have chosen lacewood for most of the deer because of its heavy pattern. This is because I intend to leave the wood natural. For Rudolph I have chosen a walnut for contrast. If I were to paint the deer I would have chosen a soft wood, and if I were going to carve some fine detail after scroll sawing, I would have chosen basswood.

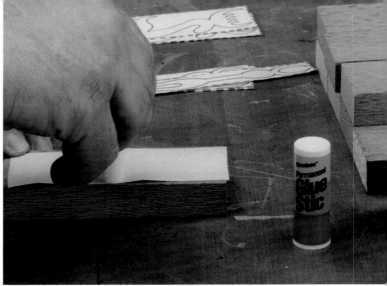

Apply stick glue to the back of the pattern. This should be a generous application.

Cut the patterns on the dotted lines.

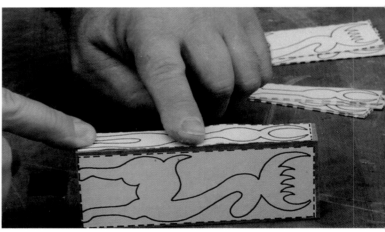

Do the same with the back view pattern. Make sure patterns align with the base, and roll out the pattern with your finger to remove any air bubbles. Set aside the block to give the glue time to dry. This gives a better bond.

I apply patterns to the whole team of reindeer before I begin cutting.

I begin with the back view, which are 2" cuts. Because of the thickness of the cut and the hardness of the wood I will use an Olson FR420R plain end blade.

The coarser blade allows you to cut without burning. This is a cut made with the FR420R.

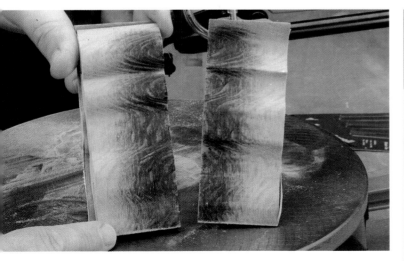

This is a cut in the same piece of wood made with a #9PGT blade. This blade is twice as fine as the FR420R, and because it takes longer to cut through the wood it builds up the heat that causes the burning.

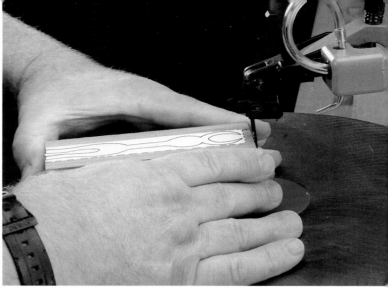

I use the saw at 1700-1750 blade strokes per minute. This is generally the fastest speed on the machine. On thick pieces like this, the proper hand position is below the top of the block. With the thick wood you can easily get pinched between the block and the upper arm.

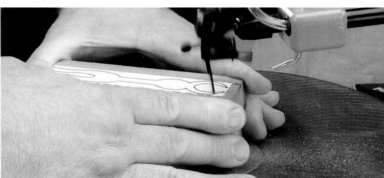

Allow the saw to do the cutting. Keep a constant steady pressure and don't force it. I do the right side first.

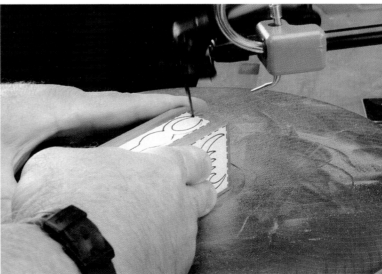

Hold the first piece in place and cut the other side.

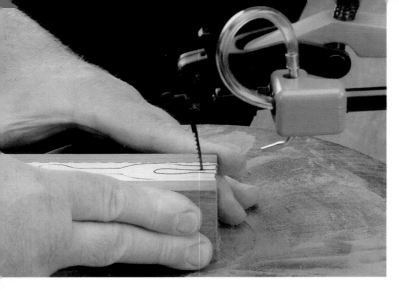

Cut out the crotch. I begin on the right side.

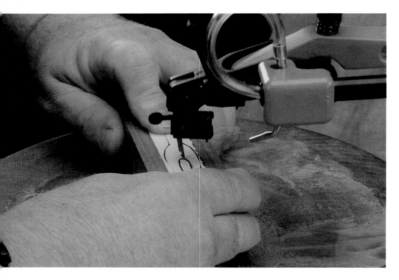

At the turn you need to switch hand positions while keeping the piece moving smoothly.

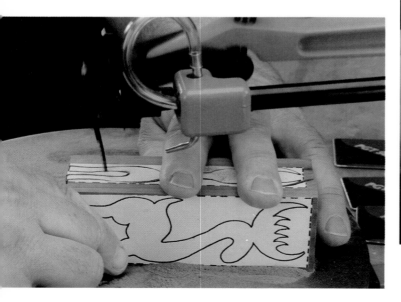

Come down the other side.

Progress. Don't cut between the antlers for now. I need this solid while I cut the profile so the antler points won't break off.

Switch to a #9PGT blade to cut the profile. Hold the side pieces in place, so they are nice and square. With the hands in this position you are touching the edge to be sure things are square.

Begin between the legs.

Before you take things apart, go back and cut between the antlers.

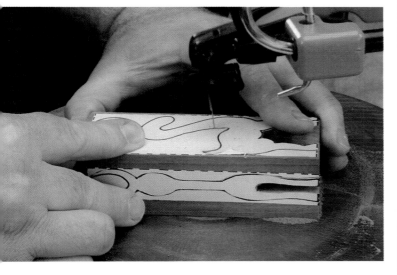

Do the profile while holding things together. You will have to switch hand positions several times. Keep a constant smooth feed rate.

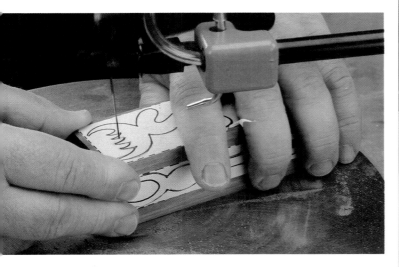

It may be helpful to practice zig-zag lines on a piece of scrap before you get to the antlers.

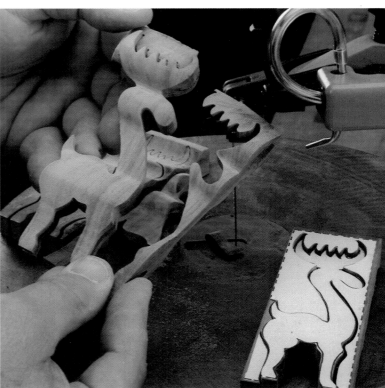

Take away the excess...

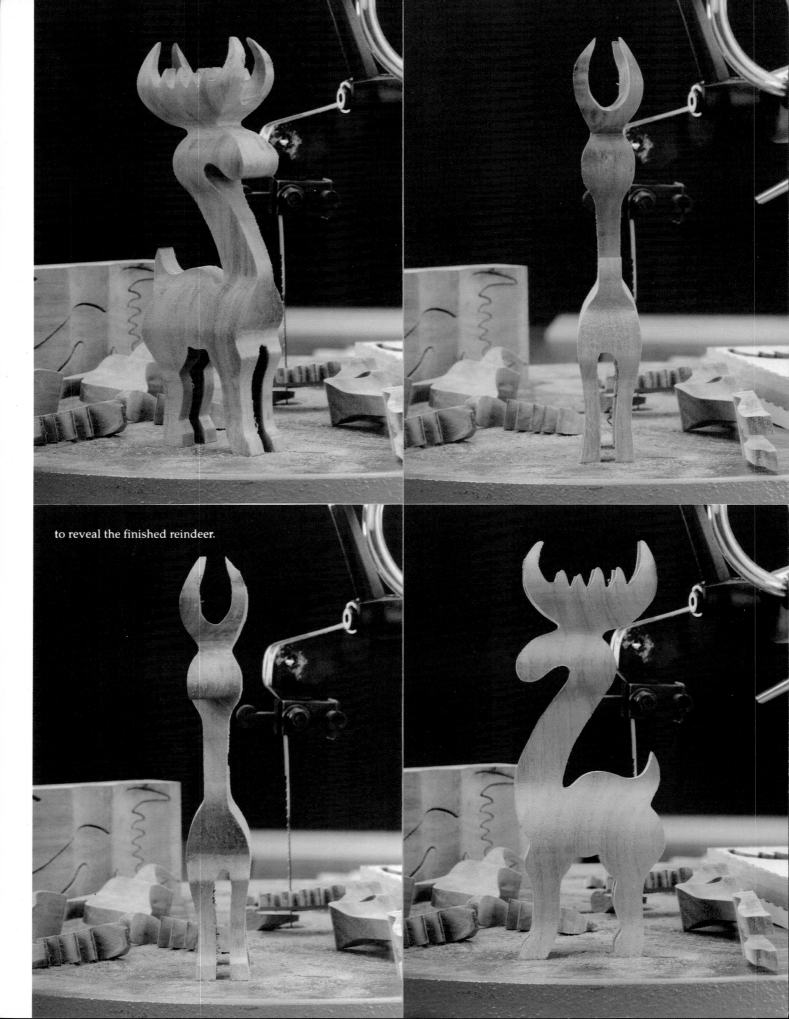

to reveal the finished reindeer.

Do the other deer in the same way.

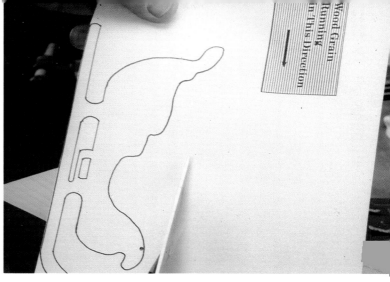

Cut the sleigh pattern. The bottom of the runner will lay on the edge of the board, so cut it on the line. You can loosely cut around the rest of the pattern.

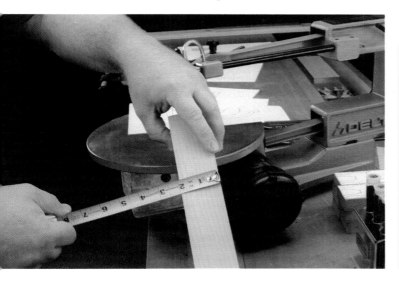

The sleigh is laid on a piece of wood that is 2" thick. This piece will be painted, so any wood will work.

Apply glue to the back of the pattern...

The pattern is 3 1/2" high and 8 1/4" long so the wood needs to be at least these dimensions.

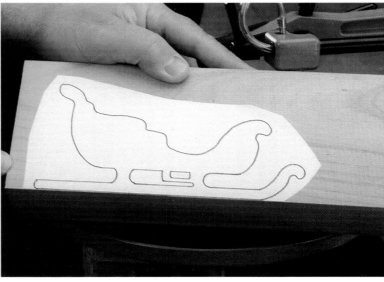

and lay it on the wood so the runner aligns with the edge and the grain goes lengthwise through the sleigh.

13

I need to drill through the openwork where I've made these dots.

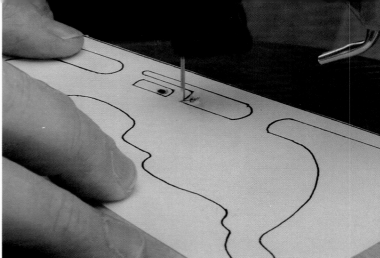

Always cut to a corner before going around the perimeter of an opening like this. It gives you a nice clean cut.

Use a bit large enough to allow the blade to fit through. This is a 1/8" bit.

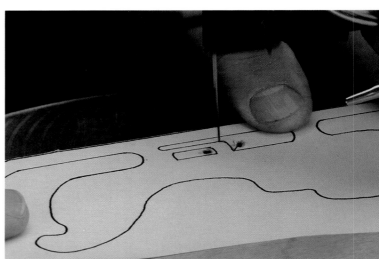

It is essential that you let the saw do the cutting here. If you force it, you will end up with a cut that is thick on one side and thin on the other. Cut around the two openings.

Insert the blade through the hole and reattach it in the blade holder, and then retension your blade.

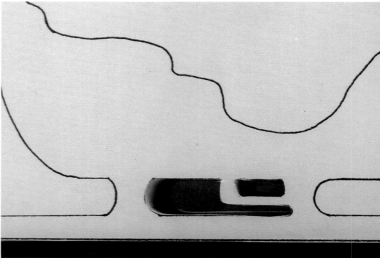

Progress.

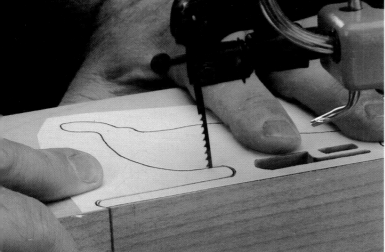

For a faster cut I've switched to a FR420R blade to cut the outline of the sleigh. I like to come in from the back and cut clockwise. Don't worry about staying right on the line. It is far more important to get a nice smooth cut.

To wire Rudolph for his red nose we need to cut off his head. I use a very fine 2/0 blade for this to get the cleanest cut possible. We need to drill a hole from the center of the nose back to here. The line is set so it doesn't come out the neck or through the back of the head. It goes in about 1".

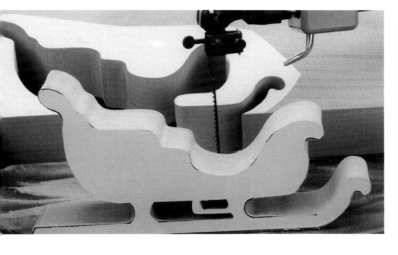

The result.

The head will be cut off here, close enough to the first line so it can be reached with a thin drill bit. The cut line is 2 3/4" from the bottom of the feet.

When removing the paper you may get some that sticks. The blade of a pair of scissors can be used to scrape it away without damaging the wood.

This is the line the drill will take from the neck cut to the first hole. It is about 1" from the cut to the intersection with first hole.

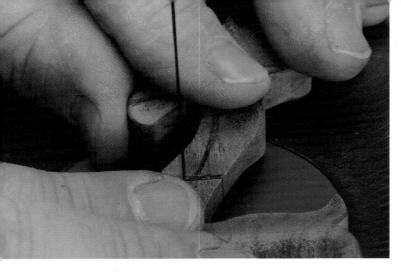

Cut off the head.

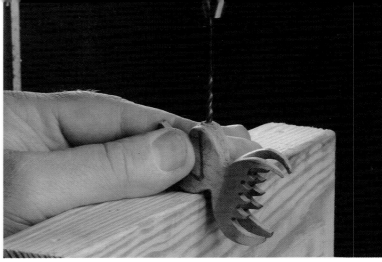

Drill in 1".

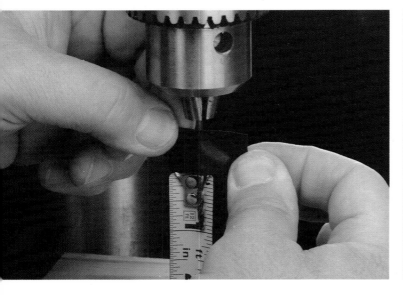

Put tape on the drill bit at the 1" mark to act as a depth gauge.

The hole through the neck almost has to be freehand. Align the bit with the angle, centering it. Slowly lift the head onto the bit.

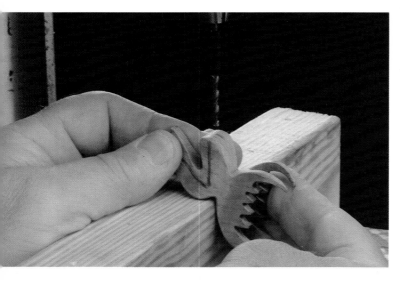

Align the drill bit to the angle you drew, being sure it is centered on the front of the nose.

It is unlikely that the hole will meet the first try, but you can go back in and auger the hole out with the bit. You'll know they have connected when you can blow in one end and have the air come out the other.

On the lower body you want to drill through the center of the neck down to between the legs.

Cut a blade back to the tooth. This will be used like a button hook to catch the loop of wire.

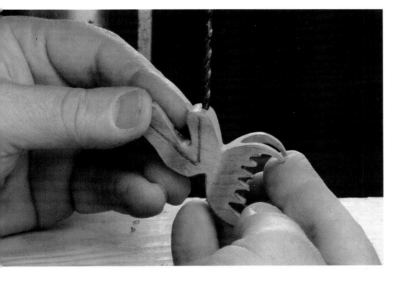

Switch to a larger bit (1/8") to widen the nose hole. This allows for the diameter of the light.

Insert it through the nose and fish for the loop. This may take a few minutes of effort, so don't give up.

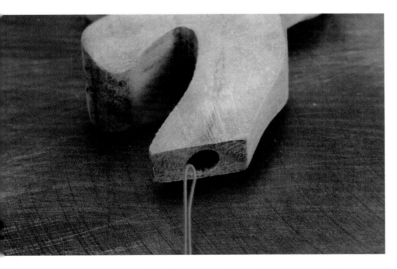

I use a 30AWG wire for the nose and music box connection. This replaces the wire that comes with the fixture. Cut a 48" piece. Fold the wire in two and insert the loop end into the neck.

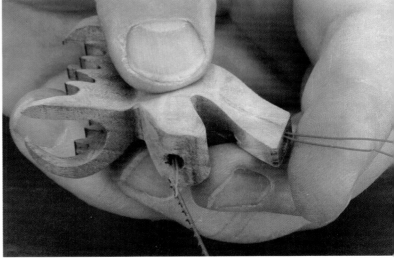

Pull the wire out through the nose.

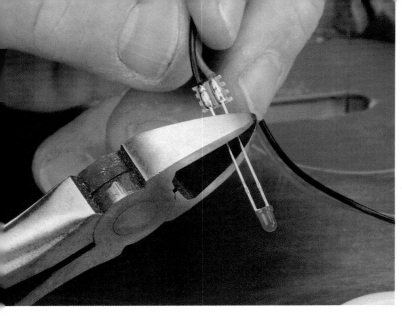

Cut the LED nose leads about one inch behind the nose.

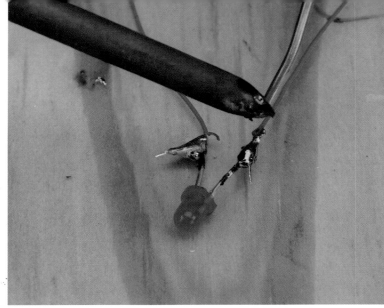

Lay the wires parallel with a twist to hold them, then solder them together.

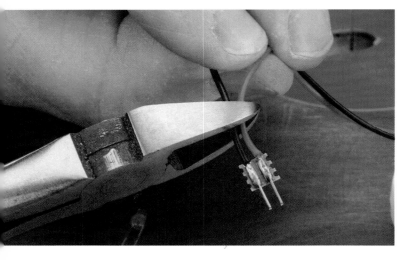

Cut the wires here.

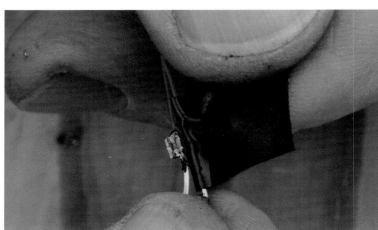

Place a small piece of electrical tape between the exposed wires and wrap it around.

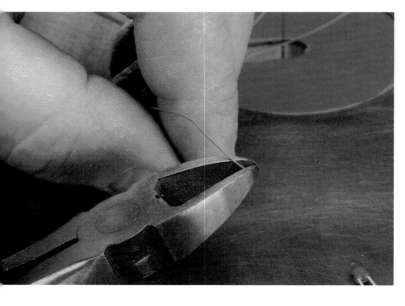

Cut the loop and strip back about 1/2".

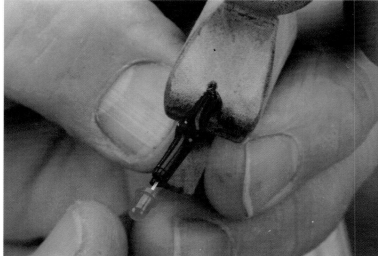

Gently work the nose assembly back into the hole.

18

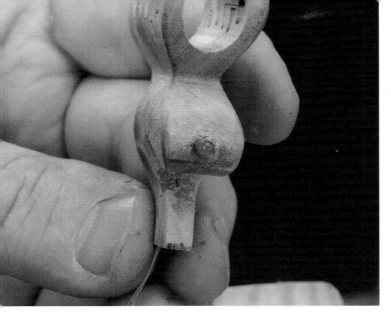

The nose in place.

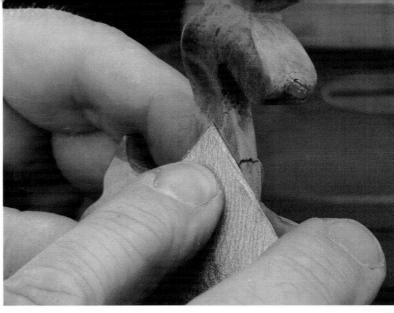

Sand the joint with 320 grit paper.

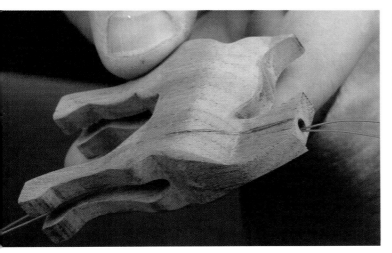

Feed the wires through the body.

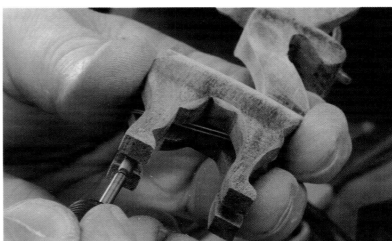

With a rotary tool or a drill, create a groove down one of the rear inside legs. This will be used to hide the wire.

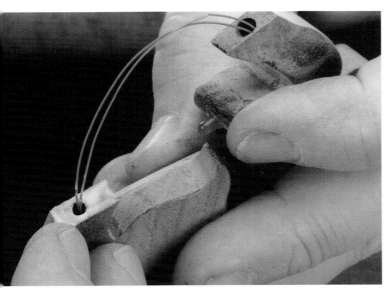

Reattach the head to the body with yellow carpenter's glue.

Here you can see the groove. The wire will be covered with a walnut wood patch fill.

This can be lightly sanded when it sets up.

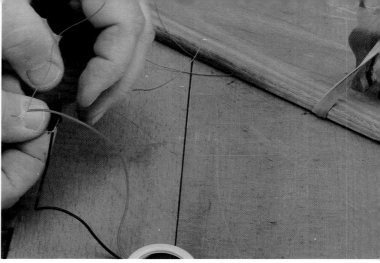

With a rubber band keeping pressure on the reindeer, I can test the wiring. It will only work one way, so find which wire goes to the red wire and which goes the black wire of music box. Mark the black wire.

Insert the wire through the sub-base.

Run the wire down the groove and hold it in place with a piece of scotch tape.

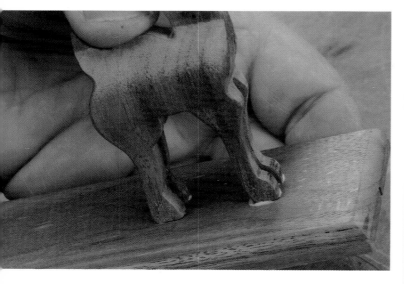

Apply yellow carpenter's glue to the feet and put the deer in place. Hold it until it sets. With the other hand clean up the excess glue. If you let it sit too long, it will stain the walnut.

Set the sub-base on the base and glue in place.

Set the rest of the herd in place. If a deer has a bad side, put it toward the center.

Roll the excess wire around the music box...

When you are pleased with the positioning, glue the deer in place one at a time. Again, carpenter's glue should do just fine.

and place it in the well.

Wire the music box to the LED. This doesn't need to be soldered. If you ever want to change the batteries it may help if it is not. By the way, the batteries are good for 2500 plays of "Rudolph the Red Nosed Reindeer" enough to drive anyone a little crazy.

Ready for finish.

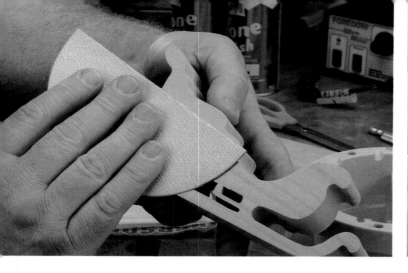

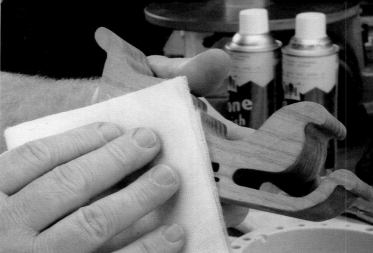

Use 320 grit paper and lightly sand with the grain. Pay particular attention to the edges of the sleigh.

Clean it up with a tack cloth.

Painting the Sleigh

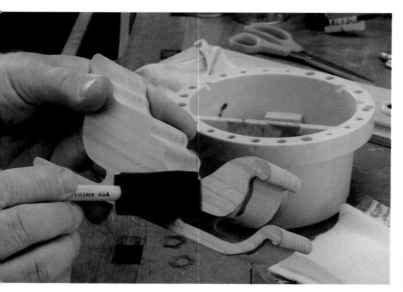

Seal the sleigh with a clear sealer.

Paint the entire sleigh. I'm using a "Christmas" red acrylic. Do a couple coats, letting it dry about 1/2 hour between coats.

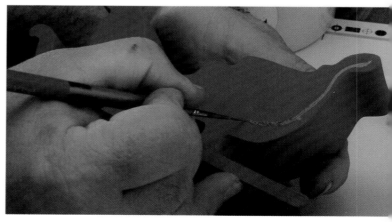

Sponge sand the sealer coat.

Accents are provided with a metallic gold paint. I begin by following the basic lines of the bottom of the cab at the front and back. You can, of course, be as artistic as you wish!

The end of the brush handle makes a nice dot at the end of this line.

By loading a toothbrush with the gold paint and spritzing it with the finger you add a nice mottled look.

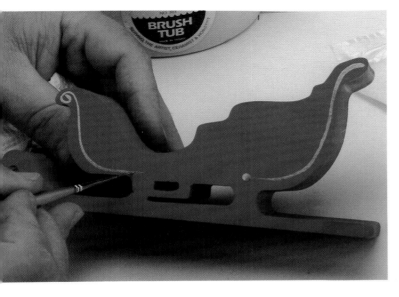

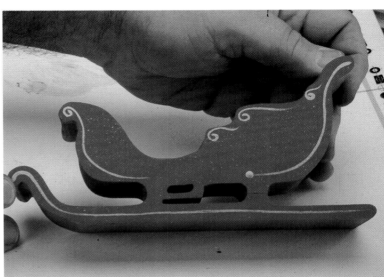

Continue to the next point.

The result.

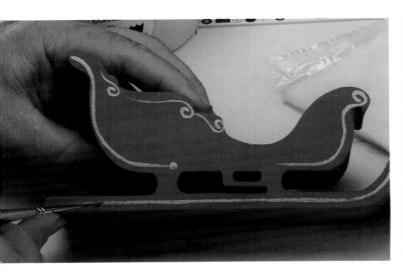

A couple swirls and a line down the runner complete the lines.

Spray the deer assembly with finish.

When you are satisfied with the finish, glue the sleigh in place.

A Santa similar to this can be purchased at most Christmas stores or craft stores. This is a 6" figure with flexible limbs so he can sit in the sleigh.

The Larger Deer

The larger pattern for the deer can be cut using the band saw and the scroll saw in the same way. I use a 1/16", 32 TPI blade on the band saw. The thinness of this blade requires that you use cool blocks on the saw, both upper and lower guides. Enlarge the pattern on a copier to the size you desire. The thickness, however, should not exceed 2" or the whole cutting process will need to be done on the band saw.

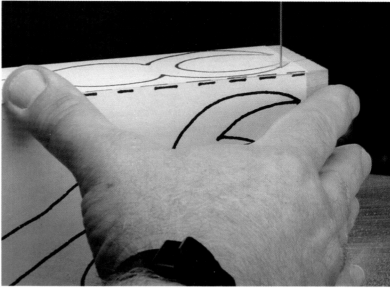

Cut the end view on the band saw, and the profile on the scroll saw. The band saw techniques are the same as on the scroll saw.

Cut the pattern and paste it on the wood as before. On these larger deer you may wish to do some carving, so choose a wood like bass wood that is a good carving medium.

A large version of the deer should emerge.

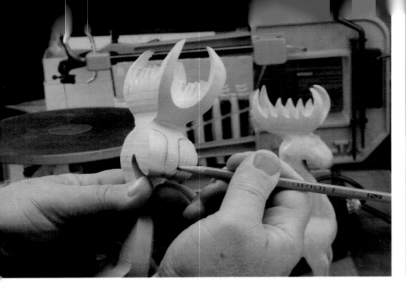

With the larger version you can do some power carving to make it appear more realistic. Draw in the nose...

With the rotary tool knock off the edges and shape some of the contours.

the ears, and the lines of the leg...

Switch to a knife to carve details.

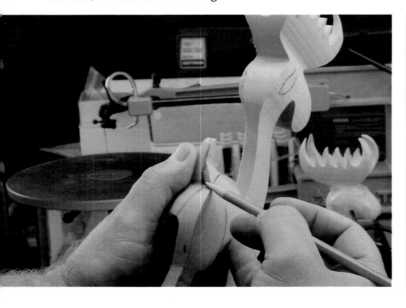

and hip.

Sand with a 320 grit paper to prepare for finishing.

Painting the Deer

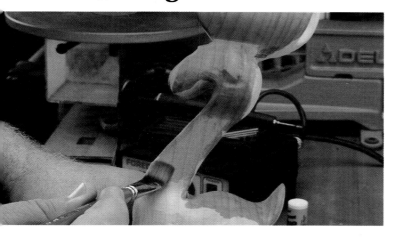

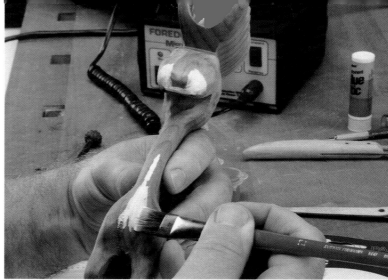

Cover with a wash of raw sienna. This makes a nice "Bambi" brown.

Continue with white around the nose and on the chest.

Paint the underside of the tail, the rump...

Paint in the eyeballs.

and the socks white.

Paint the nose black.

Paint around the eye, adding lashes, and paint the pupil.

Add random dots of white to the back.

Paint the hooves black.

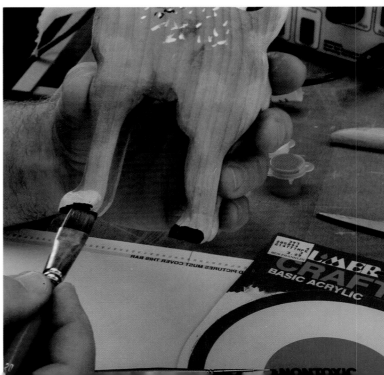

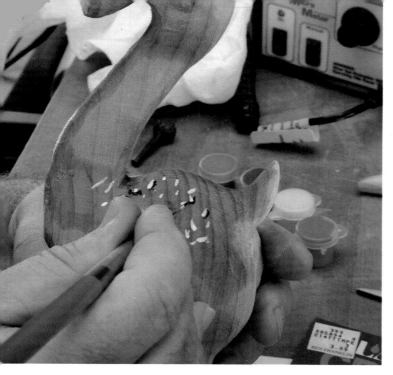

Highlight some of the dots with black.

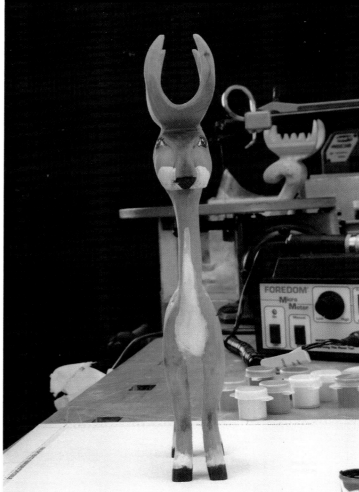

Add dark brown highlights to the ears, the nose, and the back. Blend the brown with white until you get the color you desire.

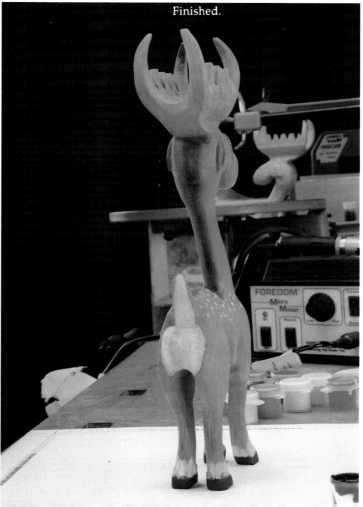

Finished.

29

The Gallery

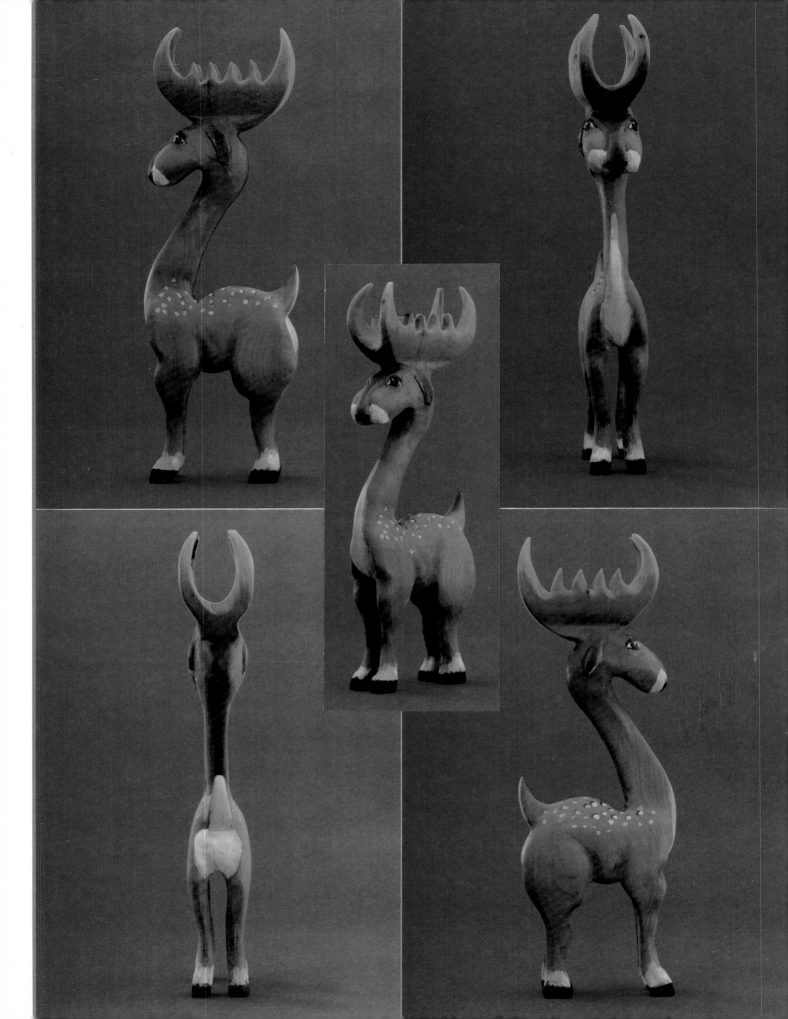

Patterns for the
Sleigh and Reindeer

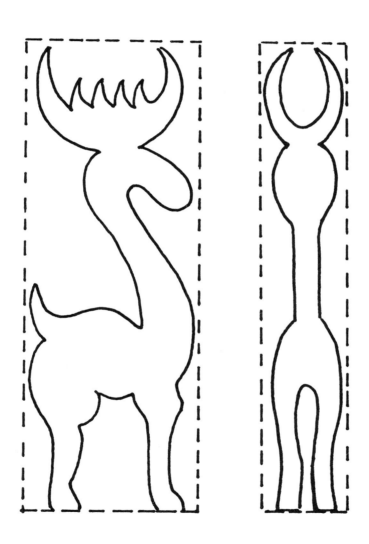

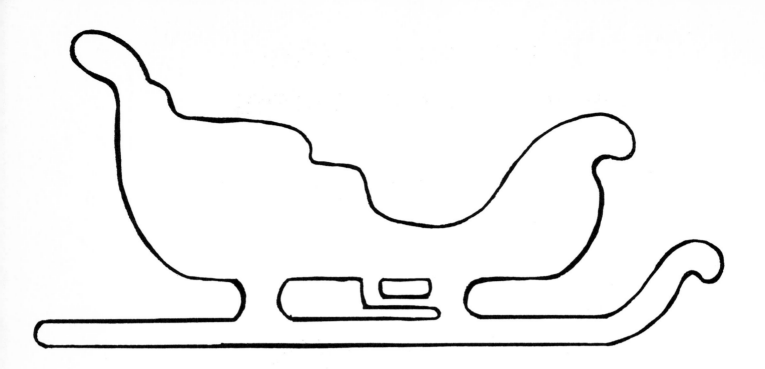

Wood grain running in this direction

→

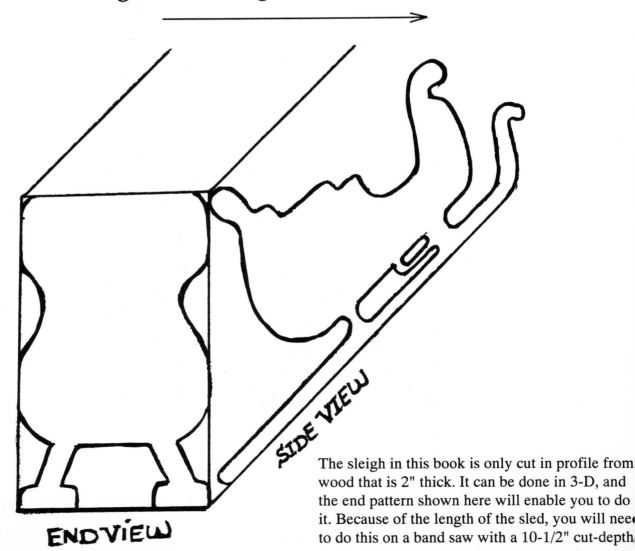

SIDE VIEW

ENDVIEW

The sleigh in this book is only cut in profile from wood that is 2" thick. It can be done in 3-D, and the end pattern shown here will enable you to do it. Because of the length of the sled, you will need to do this on a band saw with a 10-1/2" cut-depth.

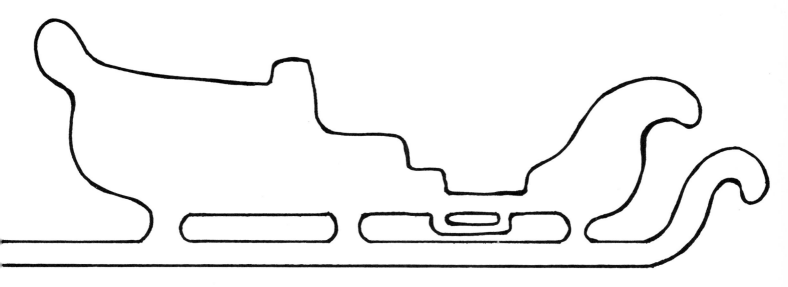

Wood grain running in this direction

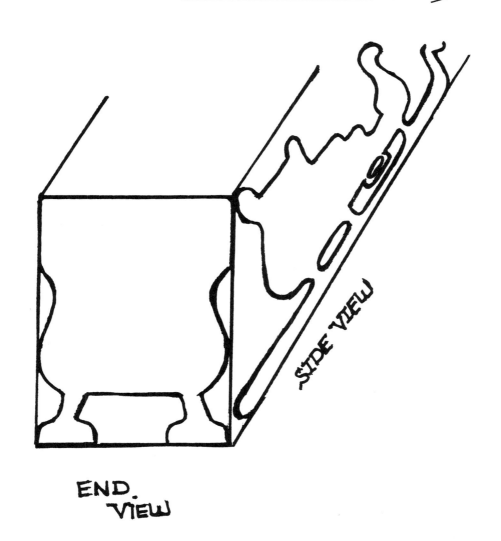

SIDE VIEW

END.
VIEW

The Storage Box

The sleigh and reindeer is rather fragile, so it I have included a plan for a storage box that will keep it safe from one year to the next.

Assembly Materials

Use yellow wood glue and small staples in an air nailer (small brads will work too). Prior to assembling the box, be sure to use a slight amount of paraffin on the left/lower rabbeted-out area. This will help make your sleigh glide in and out of the box effortlessly.

Materials
Pine

Base	3/4" x 5-1/4" x 28-1/2"
L/R lower	
rabbeted brackets	3/4" x 1" x 28"
Rabbet out:	3/4" x 7/16"
L/R upper corners	3/4" x 3/4" x 28"

Red Oak Paneling

Two sides	3/16" x 9" x 28-1/2"
Top side	3/16" x 5-3/4" x 28-1/2"
Door	3/16" x 5-3/16" x 8-1/8"
Door hinges	5/8" x 1"
Door Hasp/Lock	
(antique brass)	5/8" x 2-3/4"

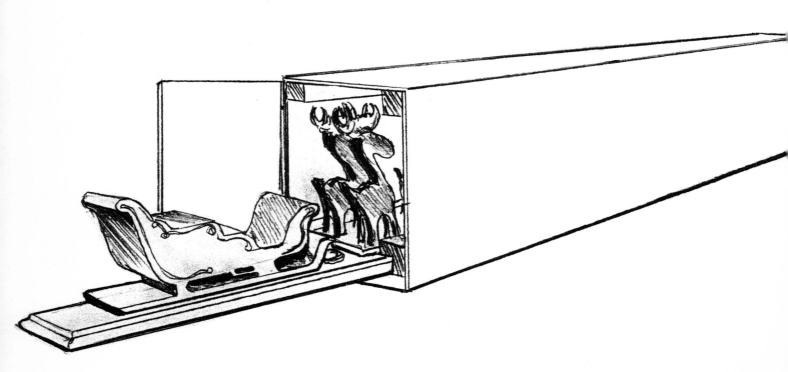

Storage Box Plan

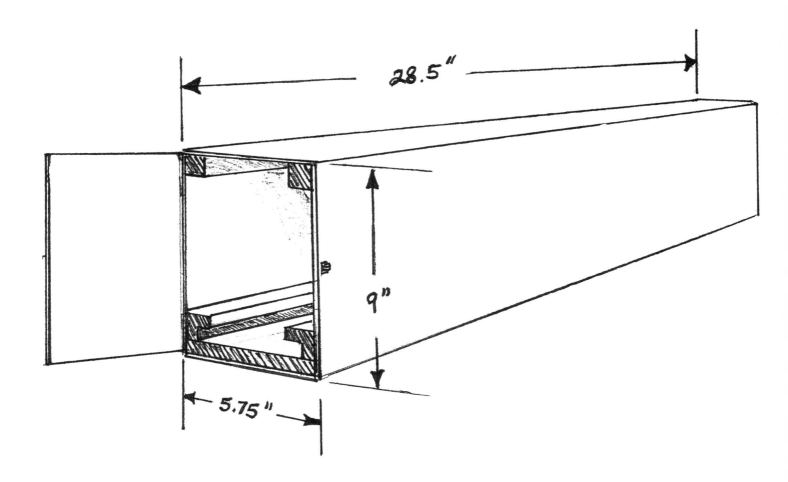

28.5"

9"

5.75"

Ornament Patterns

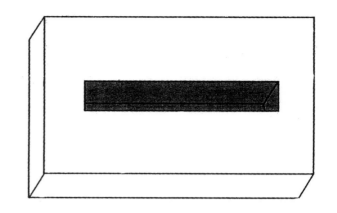

Suggested Woods

Baltic Birch: 1/8"
Aromatic Cedar 1/8"
or Any Solid Plywood 1/8"

Any of the patterns can be changed in size. Some were made for a simple cut, making it possible to cut many at the same time. Each can be painted the color of your choice or can be finished naturally.

Suggested Bases

Primarily for the *Children's Christmas Nativity* these bases are cut from a small piece of 1/4" wood.

Cut out a 1/8" mortise to fit the figure. They can be pushed into the slot and easily taken out for storage.

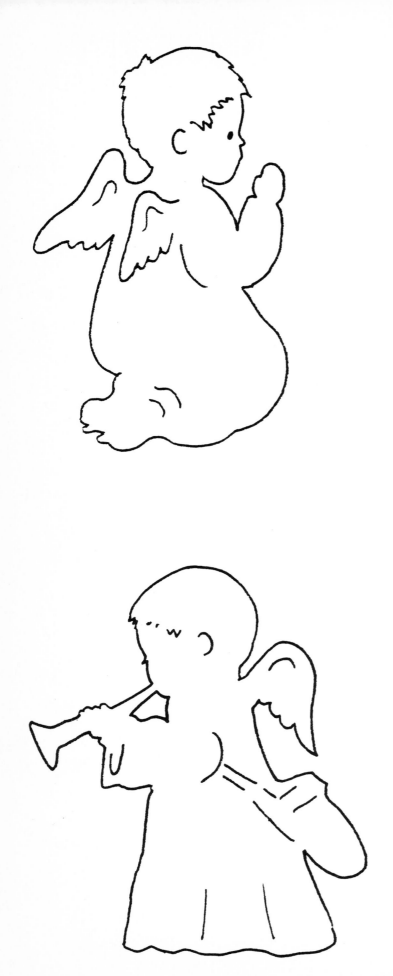

NAME

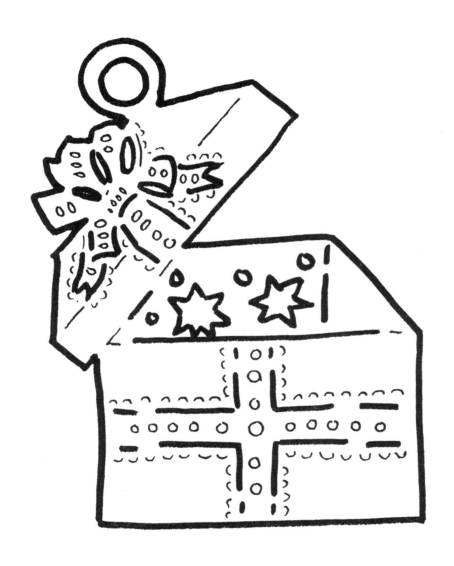

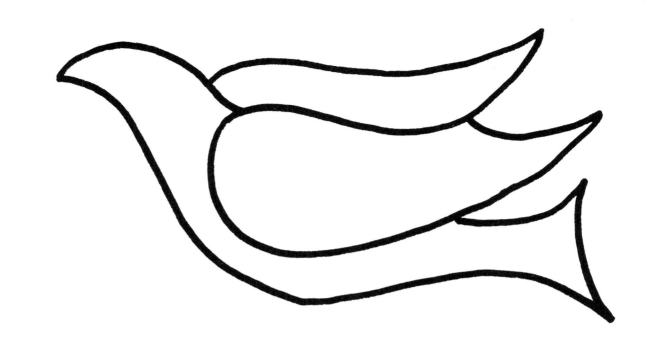